HORSE HARMONY

Understanding Horse Types and Temperaments ...
A Feeding Guide

Madalyn Ward, D.V.M.

Copyright © 2010 by Madalyn Ward, D.V.M.

All rights reserved. No part of this book may be reproduced or transmitted in any form or by any means, electronic or mechanical, including photocopying, recording, or by any information storage and retrieval system, without written permission from the Publisher, except by a reviewer quoting brief excerpts for a review in a magazine or newspaper. Requests for permission should addressed to:

Myriah Press
info@horseharmony.com

Disclaimer or Liability

The Authors and Publishers shall have neither liability nor responsibility to any person or entity with respect to any loss or damage caused or alleged to be caused directly or indirectly by the information contained in this book. While the book is as accurate as the Authors can make it, there may be errors, omissions, and inaccuracies.

ISBN-13: 978-0-9779714-2-8
ISBN: 0-9779714-2-2

Printed in the United States of America.

This book is dedicated to Cerise and Remi.

Table of Contents

Chapter One: Five-Element Feeding..1

Chapter Two: Feeding the Fire Horse..5

Chapter Three: Feeding the Earth Horse...13

Chapter Four: Feeding the Metal Horse...21

Chapter Five: Feeding the Water Horse...31

Chapter Six: Feeding the Wood Horse..37

Chapter Seven: Horse Harmony Resources..45

Chapter One: Five-Element Feeding

The Five-Element Horse Temperament Typing System

Your horse is a unique individual, and like any human, he has his own quirks and traits. Also like humans, horses can be classified into different temperament types, each with its own strengths, weaknesses, needs, and wants. Because each type needs to be managed and treated individually, I developed the Five-Element temperament typing system, which includes five basic types and six combination types. The five basic types include:

- Fire
- Earth
- Metal
- Water
- Wood

The combination types include two combinations each of Fire and Wood, Earth and Metal, and Fire and Water. To learn more about each type, please explore the Horse Harmony website (http://horsetemperament.com). This book covers feeding guidelines for the five basic types. If your horse is one of the combination temperament types, read the guidelines for both relevant types to discover how best to feed your horse.

Feeding by Five-Element Temperament Type

Although many horse owners and trainers are now beginning to acknowledge the differences between the horse temperament types when it comes to training and management, few acknowledge the need to design unique feeding programs for each type. Yet, if each type needs to be handled and trained differently, why should all types be fed the same way?

Health-wise, each of the types is prone to different ailments and illnesses. For example, the ultra-competitive Wood horse tends to suffer injuries to the tendons and ligaments, as well as being a prime candidate for intestinal ulcers. The Metal horse, on the other hand, has extremely strong tendons and ligaments, but often suffers from breathing and lung issues, such as heaves.

Luckily, by following a specific feeding program designed to bolster the health weaknesses of each type, most of these conditions can be prevented or alleviated.

The Challenge of Five-Element Typing and Feeding

Of course, to design an appropriate feeding program for your horse, you first have to know his Five-Element temperament type. You can discover your horse's temperament type with a horse temperament consultation (http://horsetemperament.com/consult.html).

After you learn your horse's temperament type, it's important to read about each of the types in the Horse Harmony book (available at http://www.holistichorsekeeping.com). By reading about each type in depth, and comparing that information with your horse's history, you can more accurately understand your horse's temperament.

While the a horse temperament consult will provide you with your horse's most likely type, a horse who is out of balance can appear to be one type while, in reality, he is another type altogether. For example, a Fire horse may sometimes to mistaken for a Wood horse. If the Fire horse is fed a rich diet but given too little exercise, he may have a Liver imbalance, which might cause him to be mistakenly typed as a Wood horse. In actuality, the Fire horse simply needs some short term Liver support in addition to a long term feeding program tailored to support the Fire horse's constitutional weaknesses.

Another example is the Earth horse who is sometimes mis-classified as a Metal horse. If an Earth horse has been over-vaccinated, his immune system can be compromised, causing him to develop respiratory infections. Since Metal horses tend to have weak lungs, the unsuspecting owner may type the Earth horse as a Metal. But in this case the Earth horse actually has healthy lungs. It is his immune system that has been weakened by incorrect management.

That's why learning more about each type and reviewing your horse's history is so important for correct Five-Element typing. Reviewing the Earth horse's history will reveal the over-vaccination, and will help sort out underlying Five Element temperament weaknesses from imbalances created by improper feeding and management.

If and when you do find that your horse does have an imbalance, don't worry. Even with the most wonderful care and management, horses can still develop imbalances because of their constitutional weaknesses. Luckily, knowledge is power. Armed with knowledge about your horse's temperament type and history, as well as the information in this book, you have the power to use foods and herbs to correct these imbalances. A proper diet will also help you prevent future health problems in your horse.

Chapter Two: Feeding the Fire Horse

Fire horses love to be at the center of attention and they want to be adored. They make excellent hunters and dressage horses, as well as good pleasure horses. They need to be told that they are loved … all the time. Fire horses are also extremely sensitive in nature, and are easily prone to stress. Feeding a Fire horse temperament type can be challenging because they can be picky eaters and will not eat simply to be nourished. Eating needs to be a pleasurable experience for the Fire horse personality, or he will simply turn up his nose and choose starvation!

Fire Horse Nutritional Support

The balanced Fire horse is high Qi, Yang, affected by heat and benefits from the bitter flavor. A basic diet should include foods which are neutral or cooling, build Yin, clear Heat and contain the bitter flavor. In other words, the Fire horse is a high energy, hot-natured horse who needs large quantities of green foods that cool and moisturize his overheated system.

Ideal Foods and Supplements for the Fire Horse

Examples of foods and supplements ideal for the Fire horse personality include the following, all of which are high in B-vitamins, making them calming and useful for the Fire horse:

- barley
- grass hay
- alfalfa hay (up to 2 flakes per day)
- wheat germ (1 to 2 oz per day)
- wheat bran (up to 1 pound per day mixed with water to form a mash)
- rice bran (up to ½ pound per day)
- beet pulp (up to 6 pounds per day)

- black sesame seeds (1 to 2 tbsp per day)
- seaweeds and micro-algae, especially chlorella (2 to 4 tbsp per day), spirulina (2 to 4 tbsp per day), and the Wild Bluegreen Mind form of wild blue-green algae from New Earth (2 to 8 tablets per day)

These horse feeds and supplements work well for a healthy Fire horse personality. A Fire horse with health challenges may need additional nutritional support. Feeding a horse by temperament type will help prevent behavior and health problems.

Fruits and Vegetables

Fruits and vegetables that fit well into the Fire horse's diet include:
- apples
- bananas
- pears
- cantaloupe
- watermelon
- all citrus fruits
- lettuce
- cucumber
- celery
- chard
- spinach
- summer squash
- cabbage
- bok choy
- broccoli
- cauliflower
- zucchini

Fruits and vegetables can make up a small portion of the horse's diet in the form of treats, or they can be gradually introduced in larger amounts to provide more actual nutrition. Any significant amounts of fruits and vegetables should be increased at the rate of ½ pound every few days. This allows for the gut bacteria to adjust to the new food. Fruits and vegetables usually have high water content so make sure at least 50% of your horse's diet is made up of grass, hay, or other sources of fiber.

Spices

Cooling spices that tempt the Fire horse's palate as well as benefit his constitution include:
- peppermint
- dandelion greens and root
- nettles
- red clover
- lemon balm
- cilantro
- marjoram

You can add spices to your horse's diet the same way you spice your own food. Spices are used as flavoring but can also have energetic effects on the body. A little bit of powdered spice goes a long way. Start by adding less than a teaspoon to your horse's food, and then gradually increase the amount. Fresh spices such as cilantro can be offered in the small handfuls. If the food becomes too "spicy" your horse may turn his nose up or try to eat around the spices. The key to adding spices to your horse's diet is to pay attention to your horse's behavior. He will tell you what he likes and dislikes.

Herbs and Supplements for Old or Weak Fire Horses

Fire horses who are old or weak benefit from herbs that act as heart tonics, as well as those that have a mild diuretic action. These include:
- hawthorn (10 cc of tincture twice per day)
- uvi ursi (10 cc of tincture twice per day of tincture or 1 small handful of leaves)
- buchu (1 small handful of leaves)
- CoQ10 (an antioxidant that supports heart function - 120 to 600 mg per day)

Herbs and supplements vary greatly in concentration and effectiveness. Suggested amounts are for the products we carry in the Holistic Horsekeeping online store (www.holistichorsekeeping.com).

Fire Horse Digestive Support

The Small Intestine is one of two organs associated with the Fire element, and for Fire horses this organ needs extra support. Fire horses are emotional and suffer from very sensitive digestion. They are easily affected by stress and diet changes. Fire horses also tend to have an acidic pH in their digestive tracts. To support the Small Intestine, the Fire horse needs prebotics. Prebiotics are substances that feed and support the beneficial bacteria (called probiotics or gut flora) in the horse's intestinal system. In addition, prebiotics help convert the Fire horse's often acidic digestive tract, especially the small intestine, to a more alkaline pH.

When a Fire horse becomes stressed, often due to emotional rather than physical causes, his normal gut flora goes out of balance, especially in the small intestine, where protein digestion occurs. This means that the Fire horse cannot properly digest proteins. His body's immune response to partially-digested proteins is an inflammatory reaction, which produces pain and ulcers in the gut lining.

The weakened gut lining allows partially-digested proteins to leave the digestive tract and enter the blood stream. This phenomenon is often called "leaky gut syndrome." Because food particles are not normally found circulating in the blood stream, the horse's immune system does not recognize them as food, and treats them as foreign invaders. These "foreign invaders" are tagged as harmful, which causes the Fire horse to develop food sensitivities, or allergies, to his own food.

Horses with food sensitivities often experience the following symptoms:
- gut pain during or after eating
- mild to severe colic
- loose manure or diarrhea
- weight loss
- refusal to eat

How to Resolve Food Sensitivities in the Fire Horse

To resolve food sensitivity issues, blood work needs to be done with proper lab testing to identify the offending foods. Once these have been identified, the Fire horse needs to be placed on a restricted diet free of those foods.

When the digestive tract has been rebalanced with oral doses of healthy gut flora, and enough time has passed to allow the gut to heal (usually six months or more), the offending foods may be re-introduced into Fire horse's diet.

To resolve a Fire horse's food sensitivities, the horse owner must address three issues:
1. reduce inflammation in the digestive tract
2. soothe and heal the intestinal lining
3. remove the causes of stress and keep the Fire horse calm

1. Reduce Inflammation

Because inflammation seems to be the underlying cause of irritation in the digestive tract, herbs that address inflammation are helpful. Licorice (8 cc of tincture twice per day) is a perfect herb for reducing digestive inflammation.

2. Soothe and Heal the Intestinal Lining

To soothe and heal the intestinal lining, feed products containing or composed of:
- whey protein
- glutathione
- mucilaginous foods and herbs such as slippery elm (1 to 2 tsp twice per day), Irish moss, marshmallow, oat powder and apple pectin
- foods that are bitter and contain chlorophyll, including AFA blue-green algae (1 to 2 tsp per day) and alfalfa hay

The mucilaginous foods and herbs mentioned above are cooling and build Yin (moisturizing), both of which soothe and heal the digestive tract. Building Yin also promotes relaxation, which is very important for the easily-stressed Fire horse. When the Fire horse is relaxed, he experiences healthier digestion and builds healthy moisture in the form of mucous, which is soothing and healing for the digestive tract. The bitter foods with chlorophyll are easy for the

Fire horse to digest, and seem to buffer any excess acid in the digestive system.

Specific products that help support and heal the Fire horse's digestive tract include:

- KLPP from KAM: provides very potent prebiotic support to create the correct environment for healthy bacteria to thrive. The maintenance dose is 10 cc once or twice per day. For severe ulcers or yeast infections give 2 ounces three times per day for 2 weeks, then 1 ounce three times per day for 6 weeks, and then 1 ounce per day for 2 weeks.
- Ulcer Formula (UF) from KAM: contains many of the soothing and healing herbs that are beneficial for Fire horses. Feed 1 tbsp 3 times per day for 2 weeks, then 1 tbsp twice per day for maintenance or until the ulcers heal.
- SUCCEED from Freedom Health: soothes and heals the digestive tract, and has a key amino acid that helps the Fire horse relax and handle stress more easily. Feed 1 ounce twice per day for 10 days, then 1 ounce per day for maintenance or until the ulcers heal.

3. Remove Causes of Stress and Keep the Fire Horse Calm

Efforts to support or treat digestion in the Fire horse can be frustrating if the underlying causes of stress are not addressed. Carefully review the Fire horse's environment, management program, and training regimen to discover causes of stress. Because the Fire horse demands to be at the center of attention, even a lack of attention from his human may throw him into a stress reaction.

Once you have identified and removed any causes of stress, you may also need to feed herbs that relax and balance the nervous system, also called nerviness. Examples of nervine type herbs include chamomile, dong quai, hops, lobelia, skullcap, and valerian.

Specific products that will keep the Fire horse relaxed include:

- Relax Blend and RelaxHer Blend from Equilite/Arenus: contain herbs which support the nervous system (follow label directions for dosages)
- Eleviv from XanGo: contains four herbs which help the keep the Fire horse relaxed and operating from the healing parasympathetic nervous system. Feed 2 to 12 capsules per day depending on level and duration of stress.

The Fire horse can be a very picky eater so these herbal products may have to be given by dose syringe, at least initially.

A typical program for digestive support in the Fire horse would include the following twice daily:
- little to no grain
- 1 flake alfalfa hay
- free choice grass hay
- 10 cc KLPP
- 1 tbsp UF (Succeed can be used in addition to or in place of the UF)
- 1 tsp blue green algae

Fire Horse Immune Support

Many of the same products that support digestive health will also bolster the Fire horse's immune system, since healthy gut flora is so important for a strong immune system. A poor barrier in the intestinal lining puts extra stress on the immune system so supporting gut health will indirectly support immune health. In addition to supporting the healthy gut flora, prebiotics and probiotics also produce B-vitamins, which help keep the Fire horse relaxed. Immune support products containing whey protein can be very useful for the Fire horse who is under extra stress or trying to overcome an infection.

Fire Horse Musculo-Skeletal Support

Natural food source antioxidants are very important in the diet of a Fire horse. Fire horses tend to suffer musculo-skeletal pain caused by inflammation rather than structural weaknesses. General body tightness can be more common than actual joint or soft tissue injury. Because Fire horses have bodies that tend to be acidic rather than alkaline, lactic acid can build up quickly in their muscles. Fire horses who are chronically stiff may benefit from additional magnesium in their diets.

Cooling foods that best address these kinds of musculo-skeletal issues include:
- Wild Earth from New Earth (2 to 6 capsules per day)

- blue-green algae (1 to 2 tsp once or twice per day)
- noni juice
- mangosteen juice from XanGo (1 ounce per day)
- alfalfa hay (1 or 2 flakes per day)

Fire Horse Uro-Genital Support

Fire temperament mares seem to be very prone to cystic ovaries, and need significant uro-genital support. This is especially likely if exercise is restricted by stall confinement or the mare becomes emotionally frustrated. The herb licorice (give 8 cc of the tincture twice a day for up to 2 weeks) works well for the pain and inflammation associated with this condition, as do herbal formulas containing Dong Quai root, which balance the Liver.

Feeding the Fire Horse

In summary, the Fire horse is sensitive and emotional, and does not handle stress well. The Fire horse is high-energy and needs to move, but is not strong enough for heavy, prolonged physical training. If confined or overworked the Fire horse suffers from digestive tract ailments. Poor digestion can then compromise the Fire horse's immune system and emotional state. Supporting the Fire horse with Yin-building, cooling, and bitter foods will support balance and good health.

Chapter Three: Feeding the Earth Horse

Earth horses love two things: appreciation and food. They are solid citizens who want to be acknowledged for the good work they do, and food treats often go a long way toward keeping them happy. They make perfect school horses and work well with children, but develop bad habits when their daily routine is upset.

Because the Earth horse loves food and will eat almost anything, he has a tendency to be an "easy keeper." He can quickly become overweight so you have to be careful not to overfeed him. At the same time, he often has trouble assimilating nutrients so you need to offer a diet rich in nutrients but low in overall calories. You must also to support his digestive system so that he gets the maximum nutrition from his food.

Earth Horse Nutritional Support

The balanced Earth horse has a lower level of Qi, is more Yin, is affected by Damp and benefits from the sweet flavor. In other words, the Earth horse is low energy, cool, subject to moist skin eruptions or edema, and does well with small portions of carbohydrate feeds such as oats. A basic diet should include foods that are neutral or warming, build Yang, clear Dampness and contain the sweet flavor.

Ideal Foods and Supplements for the Earth Horse

Examples of foods and supplements ideal for the Earth horse include:

- oats
- corn
- beet pulp (up to 2 pounds per day)
- grass hay

The Earth horse who is not working will often maintain his weight and health on grass or good grass hay with occasional vegetable treats. If the Earth horse acts excessively hungry even though he is fat, cut back on his hay and add more nutrient-dense foods into his diet.

Fruits and Vegetables

Earth horses do well with certain vegetables, which include:
- carrots (up to 5 pounds per day)
- cabbage (up to 1 pound per day)
- sweet potato (up to 2 pounds per day)
- pumpkin (up to 4 pounds per day)

Bitter Foods

The Earth horse can also benefit from small amounts of bitter foods, which help to dry the dampness that can cause problems in the Earth horse. These foods include:
- alfalfa (up to 1 flake per day)
- blue-green algae (up to 1 tbsp per day)

Foods to Feed in Small Quantities or Avoid Feeding to the Earth Horse

Foods that contribute to damp and should not be fed to the Earth horse or should be fed only in small amounts include:
- soy products
- poor quality oils
- salty foods

Wheat bran can be useful to the Earth horse since it is high in fiber and minerals, especially phosphorus and magnesium. However, it does contain some sugar so most Earth horses will not need more than a pound per day. It is not suitable for young Earth horses, but adult horses of this type can do very well when fed bran mash in place of grains.

Healthy Fats for the Earth Horse

All horse types need some source of fat in their diet, but you have to be careful about feeding too much or the wrong kinds of fats to the Earth horse, who has a tendency to be overweight. Healthy sources of fat for the Earth horse, which should be fed in small amounts only, include:

- flax seeds (up to 1 cup per day)
- hemp seeds (up to 1/4 cup per day)
- chia seeds (up to 1/4 cup per day)
- coconut oil (up to 2 tbsp per day)

Earth Horse Digestive Support

The Earth horse temperament seems to have the most trouble with assimilation of nutrients. Many Earth horses tend to be overweight so owners compensate by underfeeding these horses. It is important to feed the Earth horse nutrient-dense foods, but not feed more than 1.5% of their body weight daily. Feeding larger amounts of poor quality food still results in a horse who is too fat, but not getting the vitamins and minerals he needs.

To support the Earth horse temperament digestive system, owners need to focus on feeding a diet that:

1. offers a healthy low-carbohydrate ration that is still tasty
2. stimulates digestion
3. prevents or heals ulcers

1. Offer a Healthy Low-Carbohydrate Tasty Diet

Many sweet foods are also high in starch, so only small amounts are needed to stimulate digestion. Lightly cooked starchy vegetables such as carrots, sweet potatoes, or pumpkin can be fed alone or with soaked beet pulp as a substitute for grain. This makes the mostly grass hay diet, which is healthy for Earth horses, more appealing. Cabbage is also a low-calorie option. Mixing these veggies with a warm beet pulp or bran mash will win you great appreciation from your Earth horse.

2. Stimulate Digestion

Warming, pungent spices such as cinnamon, fennel, ginger and garlic can be beneficial in very small amounts to stimulate digestion. Supplements that are useful for stimulating digestion in the Earth horse include:

- Enzymes Plus from New Earth: an enzyme product that also contains pungent digestive aids (4 to 8 capsules per day)
- PreProbiotics from Equilite/Arenus (10 grams per day)
- KLPP from KAM (10 to 20 cc once or twice daily)

3. Prevent or Heal Ulcers

When stressed, the Earth horse can develop stomach ulcers. To soothe the stomach and speed healing, focus on feeding astringent herbs and soothing herbs, or supplements that coat the stomach lining and buffer acid. Herbs and supplements that can prevent or heal ulcers in Earth horses include:

- aloe vera: an astringent herb (1 ounce twice per day)
- slippery elm: a soothing herb (2 to 3 tsp twice per day)
- Stomach Soother by Natural Plan: contains enzyme-rich papaya, which coats the stomach and buffers acid (1 to 2 ounces per day)
- green clay: use short term to coat the stomach lining and buffer acid (1 tbsp twice per day for 10 days)

More stubborn cases of ulceration are probably related to hind gut ulceration caused by poor digestion. Digestive support products useful for Earth horses experiencing chronic digestive upsets include:

- Stomach Soother by Natural Plan (1 to 2 ounces per day)
- SUCCEED from Freedom Health: this product is high in fat so is best used short term for the Earth horse (1 tube paste or 1 ounce powder per day)

Earth Horse Immune Support

Because the Earth horse has poor digestion and is subject to dampness throughout his body, he needs a lot of immune support. Specifically, dampness and poor digestion can lead to:

1. parasite infestations
2. fungal infections

3. lymphatic imbalances
4. respiratory infections

1. Clearing or Preventing Parasite Infestation in the Earth Horse

The Earth horse is susceptible to parasites due to his tendency to have dampness in the form of excess heavy mucus and poorly-digested food in his digestive tract. Parasites thrive in this kind of environment so efforts to clear dampness not only support good digestion, but also make the Earth horse less susceptible to parasites. Frequent chemical de-worming will not clear the underlying conditions that allow parasites to thrive, but feeding the right kinds of foods and supplements can.

The following can be given in larger than usual amounts for several days at a time to help clear the intestines of parasites:

- cabbage (1/4 of a small head per day)
- pumpkin seeds (1 cup per day)
- garlic (up to 5 fresh cloves per day)

The following supplements are also helpful in reducing the parasite load for Earth horses:

- Garlic Plus C from Equilite/Arenus: creates a less hospitable environment in the body for parasites (1/2 ounce per day)
- Spectrabiotic from New Earth: a great digestive tract conditioner that can be given once or twice a month. Any horse can benefit but Earth horses are especially helped by 15 capsules per 1000 pounds.

2. Clearing or Preventing Fungal Infections in the Earth Horse

Just as dampness in people can be the underlying cause of yeast overgrowth, the same may occur in horses. In Earth horses, this shows up as a tendency toward thrush in their feet and fungal skin infections. Adding prebiotics and probiotics to the diet supports healthy flora (beneficial bacteria) in the body, and will help the Earth horse resist these infections. Beneficial bacteria support the immune system by creating an environment less hospitable to pathogen growth, as well as producing antibacterial agents that directly kill pathogens.

Specific prebiotic and probiotic products include:
- acidophilus and bifidus from New Earth (3 to 6 capsules per day of each)
- Pro-Bi from ABC (10 cc per day)
- PreProbiotics from Equilite/Arenus (10 grams per day)
- Fastrack from Conklin (1 tbsp twice per day)

3. Rebalancing Lymphatic Imbalances in the Earth Horse

Dampness not only affects the Earth horse's digestive system, but also his lymphatic system. Dampness in the system clogs up the lymphatic pathways that drain toxin-filled fluid away from the tissues, and carry it to the spleen for purification. Echinacea is one of the few herbs that supports the lymphatic system. In addition to absorbing toxins in the digestive tract, Echinacea contains a polysaccharide (sugar) that directly affects streptococcus (the bacteria that causes strangles and other milder respiratory infections).

Equinacea from Equilite/Arenus (1/2 ounce per day) is perfect for the Earth horse who is showing lymphatic imbalance, such as stocking up in the legs or swollen lymph nodes. Once the horse is exhibiting strong heat signs, such as high fever or thick yellow discharge, the Equinacea should be combined with a product such as Equilite/Arenus' Citrus C/Q (1 to 2 ounces per day) to address the inflammation.

4. Clearing Respiratory Infections in the Earth Horse

Dampness in the respiratory passages can manifest in the Earth horse as a chronic cold or a snotty nose. The herb Echinacea is also useful here, since it has anti-microbial, anti-parasitic, and pain-relieving properties. For Earth horses with chronic colds, Equilite/Arenus' Equinacea (1/2 ounce per day) is the perfect product. For general immune support, combine Equinacea with Garlic Plus C (1/2 ounce per day), also from Equilite/Arenus.

Earth Horse Musculo-Skeletal Support

Earth horses tend to need support for their muscles rather than their joints, and high-quality protein helps the Earth horse develop strong, supple muscles. The goal is to offer foods or supplements that have high-quality protein without excess calories. Alfalfa, for instance, is a rich source of protein, but is too high in calories and should not be fed to an Earth horse unless he is being worked regularly. Low-calorie sources of quality protein that are good for the Earth horse include:

- blue-green algae (1 to 2 tbsp per day)
- bee pollen (1 to 2 tbsp per day)
- royal jelly (1 to 2 tbsp per day)

Fermented products can also be a good source of protein for the Earth horse, since the fermentation process makes protein more easily available. These fermented products are ideal to feed the Earth horse in moderation:

- chaff hay
- Equipride

Astringent herbs can help remove dampness that creates stiffness. Yucca is one example, and it is often combined with the bitter herb devil's claw to make a nice pain relief product. Ani-Motion (1/2 ounce per day) is a product that is very effective as a pain relief product for Earth horses. Start with small doses and gradually increase as needed.

Finally, sulfur is a good supplement for the Earth horse because this mineral is important in muscle development and protein metabolism and has a warming effect on the body. Ideal whole food sources of sulfur include cabbage and garlic. MSM is not a whole food but is good for muscle support in a hard working Earth horse.

Earth Horse Uro-Genital Support

Dampness in the uterus of Earth mares will contribute to bacterial infections as well as fluid accumulation and cyst formation. Red raspberry is an astringent herb that dispels damp, and is included in many female tonics.

In Traditional Chinese Medicine the Spleen is responsible for keeping blood within its channels. In women, Spleen weakness is responsible for many cases of excessive menstrual bleeding. This symptom would not be seen in horses except after foaling. Vitamin C, Vitamin K, and bioflavonoids are nutrients that are considered hemostatic, meaning they prevent excessive bleeding. Cayenne pepper is a good example of a food that contains all three of these nutrients, so there is some advantage to including it in the diet of an Earth mare due to foal.

Enzymes Plus (4 to 8 capsules per day) from New Earth contains cayenne and other warming herbs in addition to digestive enzymes.

Dampness which slows lymphatic drainage can be an issue for pregnant mares. Swelling of the lower legs and belly responds to warming herbs such as cayenne as well as diuretic herbs, which remove damp, including uvi ursi and buchu leaves (feed about 1/4 cup of either as needed). Dampness in the uterus can impair pregnancy by creating and environment supportive of pathogenic bacteria, cyst formation, and fluid accumulation. Products beneficial for treating dampness in the digestive tract and supporting the immune system are equally helpful in the uro-genital system.

Earth stallions and geldings can also have uro-genital issues, such as heavy accumulations of smegma in the sheath or prostate problems. Echinacea will help with dirty sheaths by supporting lymphatic drainage, while pumpkin seeds (give 1/2 cup per day) are very good for prostate problems.

Feeding the Earth Horse

In summary, the Earth horse is a slow moving horse who should be encouraged to exercise. Foods in the Earth horse's diet should be primarily neutral to warming, support the Yang energy, and clear dampness.

Even though sweet is the flavor associated with Earth, it should not be overused, especially if in the form of refined carbohydrates. Owners of Earth horses will have to be especially careful of this because the Earth horse has a serious sweet tooth and will do almost anything for a sweet treat!

The Earth horse handles stress fairly well due to his laid back nature, but has an inherent digestive weakness when it comes to assimilation of nutrients. Feeding the Earth horse is all about supporting the digestive system while keeping the calories in check.

Chapter Four: Feeding the Metal Horse

The Metal horse is the prototypical hard-working ranch horse. He enjoys order and control, and can stand up to some of the toughest working conditions. Metal horses do their jobs perfectly but otherwise desire very little interaction. Unlike the Earth horse, the Metal horse assimilates nutrients very easily. And unlike the Fire horse, the Metal horse is not a picky eater, and doesn't mind eating different kinds of foods.

Metal Horse Nutritional Support

The Metal horse is balanced in his Qi energy, and balanced in his Yin/Yang energy which means he is not overly affected by heat or cold. He is affected by dryness and benefits from small amounts of the pungent (spicy) flavor. Because of his balanced nature the Metal horse can handle and wide variety of foods and has few digestive issues. The organs associated with the Metal type are the Lung and Large Intestine, and these are the organs that need the most support.

Ideal Foods and Supplements for the Metal Horse

The Metal horse assimilates foods very well so overfeeding is a problem if the horse is not in hard work. The goal in feeding a Metal horse is simply to maintain his body weight, while at the same time offering foods that are mucilaginous, moisturizing, and pungent. Mucilaginous and moisturizing foods and herbs help combat the Metal horse's tendency toward dryness, while pungent foods, fed in small quantities, support healthy fiber digestion in the large intestine.

The ideal diet for the average Metal horse contains whole grains plus grass or grass hay to maintain body weight. Bitter foods such as alfalfa and blue green algae can be too stimulating and if overfed will create nervousness and unpredictable behavior. Good quality fat is important in the diet of the Metal horse. Rice bran is a good fat source and feeding it will help keep the coat from getting dry and dull.

Additional supplements to the Metal horse's diet include moisturizing foods and small amounts of pungent foods. Examples of moisturizing or mucilaginous herbs include:

- aloe vera (1 to 2 ounces per day)
- burdock (usually in combination formulas with other herbs)
- dandelion (5 to 10 cc per day of tincture or in combination formulas with other herbs)
- Echinacea (10 to 20 cc per day short term for immune support)
- fenugreek (up to 2 tsp per day of the seeds)
- kelp (1 to 2 tbsp per day)
- psyllium (1 to 2 tbsp per day)
- slippery elm (1 to 4 tsp per day)
- Irish moss (1 to 2 tbsp per day)
- mullein (1 to 2 tbsp per day)

Pungent herbs are also beneficial to the Metal horse, and include:

- capsicum
- fennel
- garlic
- ginger
- peppermint
- sage
- thyme

All spices are strong and should not be given in large amounts. To provide adequate pungent flavor to support the Metal element, give 1/4 to 1/2 tsp per day of any of the above herbs or a few drops of peppermint oil.

Enzymes Plus (4 to 8 capsules per day) from New Earth contains many pungent herbs as well as digestive enzymes, making it the perfect addition to the Metal horse's diet to support healthy large intestine function. Citrus C/Q (1 to 2 ounces per day) from

Equilite/Arenus is a natural source of vitamin C and bioflavanoids, and gives support the other paired Metal organ, the Lung.

Metal Horse Digestive Support

The weakness of the Metal horse's digestive tract is the large intestine, and excessive dryness will damage this organ. Impaction colic is the result of dryness in the large intestine so monitoring water consumption is very important. Metal horses also have an extremely high pain tolerance, which can allow a mild impaction to advance to a severe problem before the horse exhibits much pain.

Most impaction and gas colic cases occur in the large intestine, so supporting this organ with mucilaginous herbs such as fenugreek (1/2 tsp per day), slippery elm (2 tbsp per day) or marshmallow (2 tbsp per day) can combat dryness that slows fiber digestion and transit time. Fenugreek is a spice that acts to make mucous more slippery while also increasing its production in the digestive track. Mucus acts as a lubricant to move manure through the digestive track. Adequate mucus also traps bacteria and parasites, and moves them out of the system.

Fats also have a lubricating action on the digestive tract and the dry constitution of the Metal horse can handle them well. Quality fats contained in unprocessed seeds such as pumpkin, flax, chia, and sunflower are beneficial.

When gas colic is a challenge for the Metal horse, pungent herbs such as fennel and ginger will stimulate digestion and decrease gas production by intestinal bacteria. Enzymes Plus (4 to 8 capsules per day) from New Earth contains digestive enzymes and these pungent herbs, so they make a perfect supplement for the Metal horse suffering from excess gas.

Electrolytes should be added to the Metal horse's food during dry weather when water consumption decreases or the manure starts to look dry. This simple precaution can be life-saving for the Metal horse. Small amounts of salty herbs, such as kelp, Irish moss or commercial electrolytes should be given during dry weather or when the horse is sweating heavily.

Metal Horse Immune Support

In Traditional Chinese Medicine the Lung is responsible for being the first line of defense against all external pathogens. Since the Lung is associated with the element Metal, it is also the Metal horse's weakest link in terms of his immune system. When the Metal horse's immune system is compromised, symptoms will appear in three ways:

1. poor skin or coat condition
2. irritated lung tissue
3. chronic lung weakness

1. Resolving Poor Skin or Coat Condition in the Metal Horse

The Lung keeps the protective Wei Qi circulating just under the skin so the overall health of the skin is a good predictor of the strength of the immune system. Dry, lusterless skin and excessive or inadequate sweat indicate weak Lung Qi. To resolve this issue and support the Metal horse's immune system, supplement the diet with natural vitamin C and the powerful antioxidant quercetin. Citrus C/Q (1 to 2 ounces per day) from Equilite/Arenus contains high quantities of both.

Over-vaccination is one of the main causes of poor skin and coat condition in the Metal horse. Over-vaccination can be devastating to the Metal horse. Metal horses do not often show immediate reaction to vaccines, but months later develop poor hair coats and skin tumors such as sarcoids. The long-term ill effects of vaccines occur because antigens injected directly into the bloodstream bypass the natural immune protection of the Wei Qi.

Intra-nasal vaccines do not cause the same harmful effects since they work through more natural routes of infection. If vaccines must be administered to the Metal horse, start him on natural vitamin C products several days before the vaccination, and continue for several days after vaccination to help overcome immune suppression.

2. Resolving Lung Irritation in the Metal Horse

Dryness can decrease the healthy mucous lining of lung tissue, making the horse less resistant to inhaled pathogens. To combat this problem, add mucilaginous herbs to the diet to soothe irritated lung tissue.

Examples of these herbs include:
- mullein (2 tbsp per day)
- marshmallow (2 tbsp per day)
- slippery elm (2 tbsp per day)

To build healthy lung tissue, especially in young horses being exposed to pathogens for the first time, or simply to support the immune system in young horses, feed natural vitamin C combined with pungent herbs like garlic. Garlic Plus C (1/2 ounce per day) from Equilite/Arenus is an excellent formula for this purpose.

3. Resolving Chronic Lung Weakness in the Metal Horse

The Metal horse who suffers from chronic lung weakness needs a slightly different kind of support than the horse with lung irritation. Metal horses with chronic lung weakness can have symptoms such as generalized weakness, spontaneous sweating, coughing, weak voice, and shortness of breath with minimum exercise. Unlike the healthy Metal horse, these horses need a very nutrient dense-diet to support the spleen-pancreas function so that the Qi can be replenished.

To support lung weakness, as well as general weakness, offer the following foods or herbs, which should be lightly cooked to increase digestibility:
- oats (1 to 2 pounds per day)
- carrots (1 to 2 pounds per day)
- sweet potatoes (1 per day)
- fresh ginger (1/4 tsp per day)
- garlic (1 clove per day)
- molasses (1 to 2 tbsp per day)
- licorice root (1 tbsp per day)

Avoid feeding large amounts of cooling foods to weakened Metal horses. These foods include citrus fruits, seaweeds, blue-green algae, and cereal grasses.

4. General Immune Support for the Metal Horse

For the Metal horse an abundance of foods and herbs that support healthy lung function will support overall immune health. Example of such foods and herbs include:

- barley
- soybean products
- millet
- carrots (up to 5 pounds per day)
- pumpkin (up to 4 pounds per day)
- blue-green algae (1 to 2 tbsp per day)
- seaweeds (2 to 4 tbsp per day)
- marshmallow root (2 tbsp per day)
- slippery elm (1 to 2 tsp twice per day)
- mullein (1 to 2 tbsp per day)
- fennel
- fenugreek (up to 2 tsp per day of the seeds)

Metal Horse Musculo-Skeletal Support

The musculo-skeletal system is another area where a hard-working Metal horse needs support. The strong work ethic and high pain tolerance of the Metal horse make him a good candidate for overuse and, in some cases, abuse. These horses will rarely complain about such things as poor-fitting tack, sore feet, achy joints, bad teeth, or adverse weather. Their stoic nature causes them to compensate for minor problems until these problems become major.

With a Metal horse in hard work it is important to take preventive action to support healthy joints, hooves, and connective tissues. The Metal horse is capable of very hard work which can lead to build-up of free radicals in the body. One symptom of excess free radicals is the thinning of joint fluid, which lowers its cushioning ability. Thin, poor-quality joint fluid leads to breakdown in the cartilage within the joint.

Chapter Four: Feeding the Metal Horse

To support the Metal horse's musculo-skeletal system, focus on offering foods and supplements rich in:

- vitamin E
- vitamin C
- minerals that support antioxidant activity, such as selenium and sulfur
- whole foods rich in macro and micro minerals
- quality fats

Sources of Vitamin E

Vitamin E is found in whole grains and seeds. The vitamin E content is primarily in the outer coating of the grain, so cleaned and processed grains will be lacking in this vitamin. The same is true with any processed seed.

Sources of Vitamin C

Vitamin C is found in whole food vegetables and fruits, as well as certain herbs and seeds, including:

- broccoli
- cabbage
- parsley
- bell peppers
- most fruits
- acerola fruit
- rosehips
- aloe vera juice
- papaya fruit (such as in Stomach Soother from Natural Plan)
- hops
- red raspberry leaves
- pumpkin seeds

Sources of Minerals that Support Antioxidant Activity

The minerals selenium and sulfur both support antioxidant activity in the Metal horse's body. Selenium, like vitamin E, is found in the outer bran and germ layers of whole grains. Herbal sources of selenium include:

- milk thistle seeds (1tbsp per day)
- buchu leaves (1/4 cup per day)
- dulse (1tbsp per day)
- pumpkin seeds (1/2 cup per day)
- chia seeds (up to 1/4 cup per day)

Foods containing significant amounts of sulfur include:

- alfalfa
- cabbage
- broccoli
- turnips
- members of the onion family, such as garlic

Sources of Whole Foods Rich in Macro and Micro Minerals

Macro and micro minerals are also important for healthy bones and joints. Metal horses benefit more from nutritive herb sources of these minerals rather than inorganic sources. Healthy natural sources of calcium, magnesium, and trace minerals include:

- seaweeds (such as Irish moss, dulse, and kelp)
- licorice root
- alfalfa
- chickweed

Natural sources of phosphorous include:

- cabbage
- chickweed
- whole grains

Sources of Quality Fats

Not all types of fats are equal. Metal horses need high quality fats to support their musculo-skeletal systems. Sources of high-quality fats include:

- chia seeds
- pumpkin seeds
- flax seeds
- hemp seeds

Metal Horse Uro-Genital Support:

Metal horses normally have very few uro-genital problems. One area to consider, though, is the interaction between the kidney/adrenal system and the lungs. Chronic stress leading to adrenal burnout will occur in the Metal horse as asthma-like lung symptoms. This condition will not respond to support for the lungs alone, since the cause of adrenal burnout. Instead, focus on feeding whole foods and herbs that rebuild the adrenal glands.

To support and rebuild the adrenal glands, offer the Metal horse rest and a low-stress environment. In addition, feed natural vitamin C and iodine-rich seaweeds, such as Irish moss. For severe burnout cases, more powerful medicinal herbs, such as those found in Eleviv (2 to 4 capsules per day) by XanGo, will be needed to strongly support and rebuild the adrenals.

While most Metal horses do not suffer from uro-genital problems, some geldings do occasionally exhibit some tightness in the flank area. Metal horses with tightness in the flank will stand with the affected hind leg forward and under the body. In geldings, this posture sometimes means that the prostate gland is inflamed, causing tightness. To alleviate this inflammation, add pumpkin seeds (1/2 cup per day) to the diet. These seeds are known to support the health of the prostate gland.

Feeding the Metal Horse

In summary the Metal horse is hard working, and needs extra support for his joints and connective tissues. His digestive system is generally good but dryness can cause impaction or gas colic. The immune system of the Metal horse may need extra support, especially if he has received excessive vaccinations.

Chapter Five: Feeding the Water Horse

Water horses need safety and a trustworthy rider. They can be brilliant show horses but panic easily. They perform well in events that call for animation and excitement, and are motivated by cheering crowds. The Water horse possesses a strong digestive system, but because of his high-spirited nature he burns through calories quickly. The challenge in feeding the Water horse is keeping him at a healthy weight while keeping him calm so he can properly digest his food.

Water Horse Nutritional Support

The Water horse has higher levels of Qi (energy), tends to be more Yang (higher metabolism), is affected by Cold and benefits from the salty flavor. Foods that are neutral or warm in energetics should be in the diet and excessive cold foods avoided.

Ideal Foods and Supplements for the Water Horse

Examples of neutral or warm foods that are ideal for the Water horse's diet include:

- oats
- sunflower seeds (up to 1 cup per day)
- sesame seeds (up to 2 tbsp per day)
- corn
- ginger
- cinnamon bark
- basil
- rosemary
- fennel
- dill

- anise
- parsley
- sweet potato (1 or 2 per day)
- citrus peel
- garlic (several cloves per day)
- molasses in small amounts (cooling in large amounts)

All spices should be given in small amounts of up to 1/4 tsp per day. Although alfalfa is considered a cooling food, many Water horses do well with 1 flake of alfalfa per day in addition to grass hay.

The Kidney and Bladder are the organs associated with the Water element so foods that support these organs are helpful. The healthy Water horse has an abundance of Yang energy (high metabolism) which helps him withstand the detrimental effects of cold pathogenic influences. A weakened Water horse can have a deficiency of Kidney Yin or Yang.

Water Horse Deficient Kidney Yang Support

Water horses with deficient Kidney Yang shows symptoms such as aversion to cold weather, cold legs, pale mucous membranes, and weakness in the stifles and low back. Frequent urination, dribbling of urine, or inability to urinate are signs that deficient Kidney Qi in addition to deficient Yang. All the above items in the "Ideal Foods and Supplements" list above will support Kidney Yang, and the addition of herbs such as rose hips, raspberry, and oyster shell support Kidney Qi.

Water Horse Deficient Kidney Yin Support

Water horses with deficient Kidney Yin show symptoms of dryness because the kidneys are not supplying enough Yin fluids. The Liver, Heart, and Lungs are the organs that are most adversely affected by dryness although all areas of the body suffer. On the other hand, an imbalance of these organs can create a Kidney Yin deficiency. Low grade fever, spontaneous sweating, low backache, and weak hind legs are all symptoms of Kidney Yin deficiency.

Foods that support Kidney Yin are more cooling and include:
- millet
- barley
- watermelon
- wheat germ (1/4 cup per day)
- seaweed, spirulina (1 to 2 tbsp per day)
- chlorella (1 to 2 tsp per day)
- black sesame seeds (1 to 2 tbsp a day)

Herbs that support Kidney Yin include:
- marshmallow root (1 to 2 tbsp per day)
- aloe vera (1 to 2 oz per day)

Water Horse Digestive Support

The Water horse has a strong digestive system, but his high-energy nature can cause him to burn calories quickly. Keeping the Water horse at a good weight can be a challenge. When under stress the Water horse will get nervous and fret off pounds at a rapid rate. When calm and relaxed the same horse can pack on pounds just as quickly.

Herbs such as Relax Blend (1 to 2 ounces per day) from Equilite/Arenus should be used when the Water horse is showing signs of nervousness. Keeping the Water horse calm will allow him to relax and properly digest his food. Proper chewing of the food helps it break down and releases more warming energy. Dental care is also especially important for the Water horse as they tend to have more sensitive teeth than the other types.

<u>Digestive Support for the Geriatric Water Horse</u>

The geriatric Water horse will need additional nutritional support because the Jing, or life force, is stored in the Kidneys. As the horse ages this energy is used up and must be supplemented with Qi derived from food. In this case the digestive energy of the Spleen/Pancreas will need extra support. Pre and probiotics plus digestive enzymes will support digestive function. Warming spices such and ginger, fennel, basil and garlic should be given in small amounts to stimulate digestion. Enzymes Plus (4 to 8 capsules per day) from New Earth provides both enzymes and the needed warming herbs.

Water Horse Immune Support

The Water horse's immune function is focused around the adrenal glands. In Traditional Chinese Medicine the adrenal glands are grouped with the Kidneys. While occasional short-term stress will build immune resistance, chronic stress will interfere with the adrenal gland's ability to release the stress hormones such as epinephrine and cortisol in a timely, balanced way.

The Effects of Chronic Stress in the Water Horse

Chronic stress will cause the adrenal glands to continuously release the stress hormones, which has the effect of triggering many damaging metabolic processes in the body. In addition to interfering with digestion and wound healing, the stress hormones drive the immune system to produce excessive reactions to normal substances.

This stress immune reaction weakens resistance to exterior invaders, such as bacteria and parasites, which attempt to enter through the skin or mucous membranes. At the same time, stress causes an over-reaction to invaders coming into the bloodstream, such as viruses or incompletely digested food particles. Herpes symptoms are due to this over-reaction by the stressed immune system. Food sensitivities are another example. Treating a virus or controlling the diet will provide only limited results until the stress reaction is brought under control.

Reducing the Stress Over-Reaction in the Water Horse

Nervine type herbs such as valerian, hops, chamomile and blue vervain can be used to calm the horse during stressful events, but if the stress is long term and the adrenal glands become exhausted, herbs that specifically control the hormone levels will be needed. Iodine is a trace mineral that supports the adrenal glands, so foods containing iodine, such as kelp or Irish moss, can be added to the diet with caution, as these herbs are also cooling. In extreme cases of stress, medicinal herbal products like Eleviv (2 to 4 capsules per day) from XanGo may be needed.

Water Horse Musculo-Skeletal Support

In Traditional Chinese Medicine, Water is the element that controls healthy bones. Needless to say, healthy bones require significant minerals. The Water horse has a need for additional minerals to keep the Kidneys capable of performing their job of bone metabolism. With the Water horse, the trick is to provide all the minerals needed for bone health without creating too much of a cooling effect. Alfalfa hay (1 flake per day) is a wonderful source of minerals, but is too cooling to give in large amounts to the Water horse.

Joint supplements such as glucosamine and chondroitin sulfate help support the joints in the Water horse, but they should not be used in place for good mineral-rich foods. Mineral-rich foods balanced with warming herbs and spices plus glucosamine supplements will all work together to keep the bones and joints of the Water horse strong.

Mineral-rich foods, including seaweeds and blue-green algae (1 to 2 tbsp per day), are excellent for bone health, but also cooling in their energy. These should be balanced with warming herbs, such as citrus peel and garlic. Healthy supplements that combine the needed minerals with warming herbs, or offer additional warming effects include:

- Four Hoofs: contains many mineral rich foods including parsley, which is slightly warming (1/2 ounce per day)
- Garlic Plus C: provides additional warming energy (1/2 ounce per day)
- MSM: supplies the trace mineral sulfur which is needed for healthy bones and cartilage, and also has a warming effect on the body

Water Horse Uro-Genital Support

Water horses often suffer from bladder infections. In Traditional Chinese Medicine, a bladder infection is a damp heat condition. An excess of fatty foods and starch in the diet can contribute to damp heat.

Foods and herbs that help relieve damp heat in the short term include:
- carrots (1 to 2 pounds per day)

- citrus fruits (1 orange with peel)
- cranberries (1/4 to 1/2 cup per day)
- uva ursi (1/4 cup per day)
- dandelion leaves (1 tbsp per day)
- plantain (1 tbsp per day)
- flax seeds (1/2 to 1/2 cup per day)
- watermelon seeds (1/4 cup per day)

These foods and herbs can be used short term for occasional infections. Chronic bladder infections are usually related to a more deep-seated Yin or Yang deficiency, and should be treated with the foods and supplements mentioned in the "Water Horse Nutritional Support" section.

Feeding the Water Horse

In summary, the Water horse can be a nervous individual who benefits from management programs that are low in stress. In addition, these horses need herbs that support the adrenal gland function. Water horses tend to have more trouble in cold weather, so the addition of warming foods and herbs is beneficial. This type horse also needs extra minerals for strong bones and joint support.

Chapter Six: Feeding the Wood Horse

Wood horses are high-energy individuals who love physical challenges, and must be kept active or they will develop bad habits like kicking and biting. Wood horses also tend to become unhealthy if they do not have enough exercise. While the Wood horse is not a picky eater, he does have a very sensitive liver and is prone to ulcers, especially if he doesn't get enough entertainment and exercise. Feeding the Wood horse is all about selecting horse feeds and supplements with few ingredients so the diet stays simple. Too many ingredients in horse feeds and supplements can be aggravating to the liver.

Wood Horse Nutritional Support

The healthy Wood horse has a high level of Qi (energy), is more Yang (high metabolism), is affected by Wind and benefits from the sour flavor. The bitter flavor is also good for the Wood horse because it helps to disperse the Qi.

Ideal Foods and Supplements for the Wood Horse

Neutral to cooling foods which build Yin and contain the sour or bitter flavor should predominate in the diet of the Wood horse. Examples of ideal foods for the Wood horse include:

- barley
- grass hay
- alfalfa hay (1 flake per day)
- wheat germ (1/4 to 1/2 cup per day)
- wheat bran (up to 1 pound per day mixed with water to form a mash)
- rice bran(up to 1 cup per day)
- beet pulp (up to 6 pounds per day)
- black sesame seeds(1 to 2 tbsp a day)

- parsley (1 to 2 tsp per day
- seaweeds (2 to 4 tbsp per day)
- micro-algae, especially chlorella (1 to 2 tsp per day), spirulina (1 to 2 tbsp per day), and Wild Bluegreen Mind from New Earth (4 to 8 tablets per day)
- citrus fruits (contain the sour flavor - 1 orange with peel)
- apple cider vinegar (contains the sour flavor - 1/4 cup per day)

Herbs that contain the sour or bitter flavor and help with Qi dispersal include:

- hawthorn (10 to 15 cc twice per day)
- milk thistle (1 to 2 tbsp twice per day for a 10 to 21 day course)
- devil's claw (combined with Yucca in Ani-Motion - 1/2 ounce per day)
- red clover (contained in Four Hoofs - 1/2 ounce per day)
- aloe vera (1 to 2 ounces per day)
- black cohosh (contained in RelaxHer - 1 to 2 ounces per day)
- chickweed (contained in Bleeder's Blend - 1 to 2 ounces per day)
- dandelion (contained in Four Hoofs - 1/2 ounce per day)
- hops (contained in Relax Blend - 1 to 2 ounces per day)
- licorice (contained in UF from KAM - 1 tsp twice per day)

Many of these bitter herbs also have a cleansing effect on the blood which lowers the work of the liver in detoxifying the system. Burdock is considered a mucilaginous herb but it also has some bitter detoxifying action. This herb, like dandelion, often grows around barnyards and should be left for the animals to eat as they need. Even though many foods and herbs can be included in the diet of the Wood horse temperament, it is best to select only a few at a time and avoid horse feeds or herbal products with many ingredients. It is best to keep the Wood horse diet simple.

Wood Horse Digestive Support

The healthier the Wood horse's digestive tract, the less stress will be put on his liver. Prebiotics and probiotics are first line defenders in protecting the liver. Any Wood horse in training or competition should have a generous serving of prebiotics and probiotics with every meal.

Acidophilus is the primary bacteria in the small intestine, and it is the most beneficial for the Wood horse. Also helpful are enzymes, bifidus (the primary bacteria in the large intestine), blue-green algae, and antioxidants. Excellent sources of these supplements are the following from New Earth:

- acidophilus (2 to 4 capsules per day)
- Essentials: contains acidophilus, bifidus, blue-green algae, and enzymes (1 to 2 packets per day)
- Essentials Blend: contains multiple strains of probiotics, blue-green algae, and the antioxidant wheat sprouts (1 to 2 tbsp per day)

Simple, low starch foods with the fewest ingredients are easy for the Wood horse to digest. Drugs and high levels of medicinal herbs should be avoided so as not to stress the sensitive liver of the Wood horse.

Digestive Support for the Stressed Wood Horse

The stressed Wood horse is a prime candidate for intestinal ulcers, so ulcer prevention products are very important in the Wood horse's diet. Useful ulcer prevention products for the Wood horse include:

- KLPP from KAM (10 cc per day)
- Ulcer Formula (UF) from KAM (1 tbsp per day)
- SUCCEED from Freedom Health (1 tube paste or 1 ounce powder per day)
- aloe vera (1 ounce twice per day)
- slippery elm (2 to 3 tsp several times per day)

These same products can be given in therapeutic levels for ulcer treatment.

Wood Horse Immune Support

The Wood horse faces two main immune system challenges:

1. allergies
2. hoof abscesses

Resolving Allergies in the Wood Horse

In Traditional Chinese Medicine another function of the Liver is helping the body adapt to changes in the environment. When stressed, the liver is not able to perform this function, which often results in an over-reaction rather than under-reaction of the immune system. This produces respiratory allergies, skin eruptions such as hives, and food sensitivities.

To clear allergies, feed dust-free alfalfa hay and chlorophyll-rich products such as:

- blue-green algae (1 to 2 tsp per day)
- barley grass (1 to 2 tsp per day of powder)
- wheat sprouts (1 to 2 tsp per day of powder)

Probiotics are also very helpful in keeping the digestive system functioning so that fewer toxins that might stress the liver are absorbed into the blood. Good sources of probiotics include:

- acidophilus and bifidus from New Earth (2 to 4 capsules per day)
- Pro-Bi from ABC (10 cc once or twice per day)
- PreProbiotics from Equilite/Arenus (10 grams per day)
- Fastrack from Conklin (1 tbsp twice per day)

The alfalfa, chlorophyll-rich foods, and probiotics should be fed year round to prevent the allergic response. Adding these foods once the body is in full-blown allergic mode may actually worsen the symptoms as the body tries to detoxify. If symptoms are present, probiotics should be started. When the allergic reactions begin to subside, the alfalfa and chlorophyll-rich foods can be added back to the diet.

Resolving Hoof Abscesses in the Wood Horse

Hoof abscesses can also be a big challenge for the Wood horse, and these can come from two sources. First, a Wood horse with weak hooves is subject to stone bruising, which can result in a hoof abscess. However, the second and more likely cause is toxins accumulating in the hoof. Stagnant Qi, along with blood in the hoof that is laden with toxins, will cause irritation of the sensitive tissues leading to abscesses.

These abscesses should never be suppressed with anti-inflammatory agents but instead should be encouraged to open with soaks in apple cider vinegar. The same chlorophyll-rich products which help detoxify the blood will greatly help prevent hoof abscesses. Adding 1 to 2 ounces of apple cider vinegar to the food can also help stubborn cases.

Wood Horse Musculo-Skeletal Support

In Traditional Chinese Medicine the Liver is responsible for smooth movement of Qi throughout the body. In Western Medicine the liver is considered the main organ of detoxification. In either way of thinking, if the Qi is allowed to stagnate in any area of the body, toxins will also accumulate there.

Stagnant Qi is the reason Wood horses suffer from joint stiffness rather than actual joint damage. Toxins accumulate in the connective tissues, and moving the Qi is often the answer rather than feeding joint specific supplements.

The Liver and Gallbladder meridians are associated with the Wood element and both these meridians pass over the flank and chest area. This explains why many Wood horses are very stiff in their ribcages, which can be mistaken for shoulder or upper hind limb lameness. The Wood horse who is tight in the ribs will not extend his front legs well or bring the hind legs up under his body. Qi-moving herbs and foods will correct this problem, and include:

- blue-green algae (1 to 2 tsp per day)
- burdock root (1 to 2 tsp per day)
- dong quai (1 to 2 tsp per day)
- dandelion (1 to 2 tsp per day)
- milk thistle (1 to 2 tbsp day)

Nourishment of the connective tissues and hooves is also the responsibility of the Liver, and products that support and heal these two areas include:

- blue-green algae (1 to 2 tsp per day)
- barley grass (1 to 2 tsp per day)
- wheat sprouts (1 to 2 tbsp per day)
- nettles (1 to 2 tsp per day)
- dandelion (1 to 2 tsp per day)
- red clover (1 to 2 tsp per day)

- kelp (1 to 2 tbsp per day)
- parsley (1 to 2 tsp per day)
- alfalfa (1 flake per day)
- co-enzyme Q10 (120 mg per day)

Apple cider vinegar will also help some Wood horses with overall body stiffness.

Wood Horse Uro-Genital Support

The uterus and ovaries are organs where Qi stagnation can be especially problematic. Ovarian cysts in Wood mares are sources of severe pain and hormonal imbalances. The Wood horse mare with an ovarian cyst will be belligerent, resistant, and in some cases dangerous. Regular exercise and Qi-moving herbs such as dong quai will relieve the suffering of mares with this condition.

The Wood mare with an ovarian cyst will not come into heat, but Wood mares can also have hormonal imbalances that cause them to have frequent hard heats. These mares are often put on synthetic hormones such as progesterone, but these hormones only cause more liver stress. Chlorophyll rich foods and liver cleansing herbs will give more lasting positive benefits, and include:

- blue-green algae (1 to 2 tsp per day)
- barley grass (1 to 2 tsp per day of powder)
- wheat sprouts (1 to 2 tsp per day of powder)
- milk thistle (1 to 2 tsp per day)
- dandelion (1 to 2 tsp per day)
- burdock (1 to 2 tsp per day)

Pain relieving, anti-spasmodic, and nervine herbs such as valerian, black cohosh, wild lettuce and hops, chamomile, and passion flower can be combined for Wood mares that suffer from alternating ovarian cysts and hard heat cycles. RelaxHer (1 to 2 ounces per day) from Equilite/Arenus is formula that can be used short term to help a mare rebalance her hormones.

Feeding the Wood Horse

In summary the Wood horse is a competitive horse who thrives on challenging work and variety. Lack of activity will often result in stagnant Liver Qi, causing painful conditions that lead to a bad attitude. Simple diets, avoidance of toxins, and regular exercise will help keep the Liver healthy in a Wood Horse. Herbs for Liver support or relaxation may be needed occasionally, but the long term use of multiple herbs should be avoided.

Chapter Seven: Horse Harmony Resources

Horse Personality Type Information
http://horsetemperament.com

Books, Audios, Ebooks
http://www.holistichorsekeeping.com/education.html

Horse Temperament Typing Consultants
http://horsetemperament.com/consult.html

Online Course
http://horsetemperament.com/class.html

About the Author

Dr. Madalyn Ward, a pioneering voice in the field of holistic horse care for over two decades, breaks new ground with her second book on Horse Harmony temperament typing. This book, a feeding guide, is dedicated to helping horse owners design feeding programs specifically for their horse's temperament type. Dr. Ward graduated from Texas A&M's School of Veterinary Medicine. She has published numerous articles in medical journals and horse magazines, including *Practical Horseman* and *Equus*. Dr. Ward has also authored several books. She maintains a holistic equine practice at Bear Creek Veterinary Clinic in Texas.

www.ingramcontent.com/pod-product-compliance
Lightning Source LLC
Chambersburg PA
CBHW080528110426
42742CB00017B/3271